WHAT REALLY HAPPENED
TO THE DINOSAURS?

WHAT REALLY HAPPENED TO THE DINOSAURS?

by Daniel Cohen

illustrated by Haru Wells

E. P. Dutton   New York

Library of Congress Cataloging in Publication Data

Cohen, Daniel   What really happened to the dinosaurs?
Bibliography: p.
SUMMARY: Explores possible answers to the riddle of
how and why dinosaurs disappeared from the earth.
1. Dinosauria—Juvenile literature.   [1. Dinosaurs]
I. Wells, Haru.   II. Title.
QE862.D5C63   568'.19   77–7545   ISBN: 0-525-42472-5

Published in the United States by E. P. Dutton, a Division
of Sequoia-Elsevier Publishing Company, Inc., New York

Published simultaneously in Canada by Clarke,
Irwin & Company Limited, Toronto and Vancouver

Editor: Ann Troy   Designer: Riki Levinson

Printed in the U.S.A.
10 9 8 7 6 5 4 3 2

To L. Sprague de Camp,
whom I have always admired

CONTENTS

WHAT REALLY HAPPENED
TO THE DINOSAURS?

duckbill

pterosaur

ichthyosaur

Tyrannosaurus

Brontosaurus

Elasmosaurus

Coelophysis

Stegosaurus

I   The Problem

You have never seen a living dinosaur. You have seen pictures of dinosaurs, and models of dinosaurs. At the museum you have seen the bones of dinosaurs.

But you have never seen a dinosaur in the zoo and you never will. Dinosaurs are extinct. They all died out a very long time ago.

Perhaps you have also seen movies or cartoons that show people finding some sort of "lost land" filled with dinosaurs. Other movies and cartoons show cavemen living in a world with dinosaurs.

Both of these ideas are pure fiction. No human being who is alive now, or who has ever been alive, has seen a living dinosaur.

Human beings, or ancestors of human beings, have been

on the earth for 3 or 4 million years. The dinosaurs have been dead and gone for at least 70 million years.

What really happened to the dinosaurs? That is the problem, because no one is really sure. The disappearance of the dinosaurs is one of the most intriguing scientific mysteries around today. In this book we are going to explore some of the possible answers to that riddle.

First, though, let's see how we know the dinosaurs are really extinct. As we said, no one has ever seen a living dinosaur. In fact, up until about 150 years ago, no one had any idea that there ever had been such animals as dinosaurs at all.

Every once in a while people found dinosaur bones, but didn't know what they were. That is what happened to William Clark, co-leader of the famous Lewis and Clark Expedition which first explored the entire northwestern section of the North American continent.

On July 25, 1806, Clark chipped a large bone out of the rocks on the south bank of the Yellowstone River below what is now Billings, Montana. The bone was three feet long and several inches around, yet Clark merely described it as "the rib of a fish." Later this bone proved to be the rib of a dinosaur.

Scientists began putting together information on accidental finds such as the one made by Clark. When the scientists had enough information, they concluded that the earth had once been inhabited by a large variety of land-living animals, some of which were gigantic. The animals were thought to be reptiles, similar to lizards.

To these reptiles the scientists gave the name "dinosaur."

The name means "terrible lizard," and it isn't really correct, for reasons we will explain in the next chapter. But the name dinosaur has stuck anyway.

The world was astonished and fascinated by the discovery of the dinosaurs. Today we are still astonished and fascinated by dinosaurs. They were the largest animals that ever lived on the land. And the strangest looking.

How do we know when the dinosaurs lived, and when they died out? We are able to date the remains of dinosaurs, or other living things, from the layer of the earth's crust in which their remains, or fossils, are found.

There are several types of rocks, but not all of them contain fossils. Fossils are found in sedimentary rocks. These rocks are, as the name indicates, formed from sediments. The sediments—sand, mud, or other loose materials—are deposited on the bottoms of lakes, rivers, oceans, or on dry land. When living things die, their remains may be trapped in the sediment. Over thousands of years the sediments harden into rock. The remains undergo a chemical change. They become part of the rock. But they retain their original shape.

Sedimentary rocks occur in layers, or strata. The newer layers are piled on top of the older ones. The deeper the rocks, the older they are likely to be. Geologists, those scientists who study the surface of the earth, have been able to figure out approximately when these different strata were laid down.

The fossil remains of living things are found embedded within a particular layer. This indicates that the animals or plants had been alive at the time the layer was formed. In this way, the history of the earth is reckoned by the layering of the sedimentary rocks of the earth's crust. This is called geological time, or the geological clock.

Geological time is divided and subdivided into units, just as we ordinarily divide the year into months, days, and weeks. These various units of geological time have also been given names.

Dinosaur remains begin appearing in rocks formed late in the period that scientists call the Triassic. By the next geological period, the Jurassic, dinosaur remains are numerous. For over 100 million years there is an abundance of evidence of dinosaurs.

Then at the end of the period called the Cretaceous (cra-TAY-shus), dinosaur fossils are no longer found. Rocks formed from the end of the Cretaceous to the present day—a period of about 70 million years—contain no dinosaur bones at all.

For over 150 years now scientists have been looking for evidence that dinosaurs lived more recently. They have found nothing. It is safe to assume that the dinosaurs died out at the end of the Cretaceous period.

Geological time deals in millions of years. From it we can get a general picture of about when things happened, but there are no details. We cannot determine exactly when the Jurassic began, or when the Cretaceous ended. Therefore we cannot be sure whether the dinosaurs died out over a period of a hundred thousand years or overnight.

All that we can be sure of is that they did die out. Throughout the history of the earth many animals have become extinct. But the death of all the dinosaurs in one period, even over one hundred thousand years, seems very peculiar. Which brings us right back to the question of why.

Often we hear that the dinosaurs got "too big" or were "too clumsy," and that's why they died out. The word dinosaur has almost become an insult. When we want to describe something as being overgrown and not working very well, we might call it a "dinosaur." But that isn't really being fair to the dinosaurs. In the next chapter we will look at some surprising things about them.

II   Myths About Dinosaurs

Dinosaurs are badly misunderstood. We are going to clear up some of these myths and misunderstandings.

The first, and most persistent, myth is that the dinosaurs were just giant lizards. Both lizards and dinosaurs are classed as reptiles. But that is as far as the relationship goes.

The dinosaurs' closest living relative among the reptiles is probably the crocodile. And that relationship isn't very close either.

Recently some scientists have even begun to question whether dinosaurs should really be classed as reptiles at all. We will look into this theory in a later chapter. But most scientists today still believe that dinosaurs were reptiles. For the moment let's accept that.

It is even wrong to say that dinosaurs were all giants. Most of them were very large, that is true. But not all of them were.

When we say dinosaur, we think first of a huge creature with a heavy body, long neck, small head, and long tapering tail. It is a creature we call the Brontosaurus (bron-toe-SAWR-us). The name means "thunder" and, yes, "lizard" again.

The Brontosaurus is no more of a lizard than any other dinosaur. The Brontosaurus was huge, over 85 feet long. But it wasn't the largest of the dinosaurs. That title could be split between two other dinosaurs which resembled Brontosaurus.

Diplodocus (di-PLOD-o-kus), a longer version of Brontosaurus, may have reached a length of 100 feet from nose to tail. Three of them would stretch across a football field. Brachiosaurus (bra-kee-o-SAWR-us) was probably the heaviest. Its top weight has been estimated as 100 tons. It would take more than sixteen of the largest elephants to equal one Brachiosaurus in weight. All of these dinosaurs were called sauropods (SAWR-o-pods). The name means "lizard-footed."

None of these great dinosaurs match some modern whales in size or weight. But they were far and away the largest land-living animals that ever existed.

Brontosaurus, Diplodocus, and Brachiosaurus were all plant eaters. The largest meat eater was Tyrannosaurus (tie-ran-o-SAWR-us). It had an over-all length of just under 50 feet. It walked on two legs and stood about 20 feet tall. Its skull alone was four feet long, and its teeth at least six inches long.

The giant dinosaurs have always attracted the most attention. That is natural. But the remains of a large number of small dinosaurs have also been found. Among some of the earliest known dinosaurs was Coelophysis (see-LO-fis-iss), which was

only 8 or 10 feet long, and extremely light. It weighed no more than 40 or 50 pounds. There were dinosaurs much smaller than that. Compsognathus (komp-SOG-na-thus), which lived at the same time as the giant Brontosaurus, was no larger than a chicken. Like Coelophysis, Compsognathus was a lightly built two-legged meat eater. It probably ate a lot of insects too. Dinosaurs came in all sizes and all shapes.

Another common belief about dinosaurs is that they were slow and clumsy. Since no one has ever seen a living dinosaur, we can only guess as to how they moved. There are several reasons to believe that they were slow.

We know that large, heavy animals like elephants are slower and less agile than smaller, more lightly built animals like deer. The giant dinosaurs clearly were large and heavy. Some scientists even doubt that the really huge dinosaurs like Brachiosaurus could have walked about on dry land. They think that the animals' bones were not strong enough to support all their weight. They suggest that the animals stayed in swamps or shallow lakes. There the water would have buoyed up their huge bodies. Their legs would then not have had to carry all of the weight.

The predatory dinosaurs, those who killed and ate other animals, were not nearly as large as the plant eaters. But many were still enormous. Most scientists think that the large predators like Tyrannosaurus did not have great speed. The animals that Tyrannosaurus ate were even larger and slower.

But as we just saw, not all the dinosaurs were large and heavy. The smaller, lighter dinosaurs could have moved quickly. Most scientists think that they did. But only for short periods.

This brings us to the second reason why most scientists think that dinosaurs moved slowly. They believe dinosaurs were reptiles. Have you ever watched a large alligator at the zoo? Most of the time it does not move at all. When it does move, it is usually very slowly.

Turtles, which are also reptiles, are famous for being slow. The larger the turtle, the more slowly it seems to move.

Some of the smaller snakes and lizards can move very quickly. But even they only show speed in short bursts. Most of the time they are motionless.

So there are good reasons for believing that the very largest of dinosaurs were slow-moving and clumsy, and smaller ones may have been too. But we cannot be sure.

Dinosaurs also have the reputation of being stupid. That is because they had very small brains compared to the enormous size of their bodies. The giant Brontosaurus had a brain only a little larger than your fist. The small-brain record is probably held by an armored dinosaur called Stegosaurus (steg-o-SAWR-us). This strange-looking creature reached a length of up to 30 feet, and weighed two tons. Its brain was the size of a plum, and weighed 2½ ounces.

Stegosaurus also had a bundle of nerve tissue in its pelvic area. This led some people to think that the creature had two brains. This nerve bundle may have helped the animal control its huge body, but it was not really a second brain.

Many dinosaurs were also heavily armored. Stegosaurus had a double row of plates running down its back. Scientists are not sure what these were used for. They were probably used for defense. It also had a clump of long spikes on the end of its tail. The spiked tail would certainly have made a good weapon. It would have helped to discourage the large predatory dinosaurs.

There was also a large family of dinosaurs called duck-bills. In addition to their duck-like faces, many of them had strangely shaped crests on the tops of their heads. What these crests were used for is still a mystery to scientists.

All of this—the size, the slowness, the small brains, and the strange and exotic shapes—has led to the impression that the dinosaurs were somehow "doomed" to extinction. One hears that they were too large or clumsy or overspecialized to survive. But such an impression simply does not fit the facts.

For over 100 million years dinosaurs were the dominant form of life on land. Even in terms of the long history of life on this planet, 100 million years is a long time. Our own ancestors began evolving a mere 3 or 4 million years ago. Fully modern man did not appear until less than two hundred thousand years ago. When compared to the history of the human race, the dinosaurs were extremely successful, and we are mere upstarts.

Of course, there were many different kinds of dinosaurs. Only a few of them have been described here. During the long period of dinosaurian dominance, some types of dinosaurs died out. By the late Cretaceous, the gigantic sauropods like Brontosaurus had already vanished. Stegosaurus was long gone. But Tyrannosaurus was still around. So were the duck-billed dinosaurs and many, many others. They were, as far as we can tell, all flourishing. Then all at once, it seems, they disappeared.

Some people think that the dinosaurs were around for too long, that the whole race of dinosaurs somehow "got old" and that is why they became extinct. Individual animals, whether dinosaurs, dogs, herring, or human beings, are born, mature, grow old, and die. But whole species do not follow the same path.

Some types of animals die out very quickly if they prove to be poorly adapted to their world or if their world changes too much. Others continue virtually unchanged for millions of years. Living in the world today are a number of animal species that were old when the dinosaurs first emerged. The horseshoe crab is such an animal. The modern opossum is remarkably similar to animals that lived in the days of the dinosaurs.

So the dinosaurs didn't just die out because they were too big or too stupid or too old. They died out for a reason or reasons. But what were they? Most scientists have looked for the answer in changes in the dinosaurs' world.

III The Dinosaurs' World

What was the world like when the dinosaurs were alive? The answer to that question may give us clues to solving the mystery of why the dinosaurs died out.

But the question is more difficult than it first sounds. Dinosaurs were around for a long time. During the millions of years that they existed the world changed a great deal. They lived all over the world, and different places had different conditions.

By studying the rocks and the fossils that they contain, scientists can, in a general sort of way, determine ancient climates and landscapes. But once again we must remember that we are talking about things that happened many millions of years ago. Our record in the layers of earth is very imperfect. There is, as we shall see, plenty of room for disagreement.

The dinosaurs began to emerge during the Triassic period. That was over 200 million years ago. In Triassic times there was probably more land above the surface of the waters than there is today. The earth's temperature was also somewhat higher. The early dinosaurs appear to have flourished in jungles and swampy areas and along the shores of lakes and banks of rivers.

Naturally the dinosaurs were not alone in the world. There were amphibians, which were more primitive than the reptiles. They had to spend much of their time in the water. There were reptiles other than dinosaurs. Early ancestors of the modern turtles have been found. Among the most interesting reptiles were the therapsid (the-RAP-sid) reptiles. They are often called the mammal-like reptiles. They are the distant ancestors of modern mammals. So both early mammals and early dinosaurs appeared in the world at about the same time.

The next period of geological time is the Jurassic. It lasted about 45 million years. Evidence indicates that there was a slight drop in world temperatures at the beginning of this period. That was followed by a rise in temperatures and a long period when the surface of the earth and the climate remained the same.

In today's world, the continents have gigantic mountain ranges, and large regions of high planes. By comparison, the Jurassic landscape was dull and monotonous. Today's mountain ranges simply did not exist. Temperatures were higher than they are now and did not change as much during the year.

Many of today's continental areas were covered with warm, shallow tropical seas in Jurassic times. A great sea covered western North America. Northern Europe, now a cold and

often mountainous land, was a tropical ocean fringed with coral reefs.

This was the time in which the dinosaurs came to dominate the land areas of the earth. During the Jurassic period the largest of the dinosaurs, the 30- and 40-ton Brontosaurus, and other sauropods lived in the rivers and swamps. In drier regions stegosaurs fed upon the leaves. Tyrannosaurus had not yet appeared on the scene, but a number of only slightly smaller near relatives preyed upon the plant-eating giants. In addition to the giants there were a host of smaller dinosaurs, both plant eater and meat eaters.

While the dinosaurs dominated the land, other gigantic reptiles swam in the earth's abundant seas. These creatures have often been called seagoing dinosaurs. This is misleading because the dinosaurs and the marine reptiles were not directly related.

Although there were many marine reptiles in Jurassic times, they fall into three general groups. The ichthyosaurs (IK-thee-o-sawrs) were the most fish-like in appearance. In life they probably resembled the porpoise more than any other modern creature. Most species averaged under 30 feet in length, but a few specimens have been found that reached 50 feet.

The plesiosaurs (PLEEZ-ee-o-sawrs) have been described as looking like a snake threaded through a turtle. The description is a fairly good one if we think of the turtle as not having a shell but merely a thick, fleshy body. One type of plesiosaur, Elasmosaurus (ee-laz-mo-SAWR-us), had an enormous flexible neck. It probably caught its prey by coiling its neck and darting its head out at great speed, in a snake-like motion.

The third type of marine reptiles consisted of the mosasaurs (MOZE-a-sawrs). They had tapering bodies and four broad, paddle-like flippers. Their heads were large, with pointed snouts and big mouths filled with fierce-looking teeth. Some specimens reached a length of 30 feet. Fragmentary remains of others indicate they might have been much bigger.

Since reptiles dominated the land and sea in Jurassic times, it might be assumed that they dominated the skies as well, and they did. These flying reptiles were called pterosaurs (TAIR-o-sawrs). Most pterosaurs were comparatively small, but one specimen found recently in Texas had a wingspread of 51 feet. Its wings were the length of a subway car. That made it far and away the largest flying creature ever.

The pterosaurs were very lightly built. They had hollow bones like modern birds. Some scientists have questioned whether these creatures could truly fly. It has been suggested that they merely glided, using their wings to catch air currents. Most scientists, however, believe that the pterosaurs had mastered true flight.

The dinosaurs, marine reptiles, and pterosaurs are very strange creatures to us today. But in Jurassic times there were more familiar creatures too. Turtles, lizards, and possibly snakes were already in existence. Jurassic jungles were teeming with a variety of little furry mammals, no larger than modern mice or rats.

There was also the famous Archaeopteryx (ar-kee-OP-ter-iks). In general structure this creature looked like a reptile. But an especially good fossil found in Germany in 1861 showed that the creature was covered with feathers. Archaeopteryx is

generally considered a creature halfway between reptiles and birds.

The next period of earth history is called the Cretaceous. It is the period in which we are really interested, because at the end of it all the dinosaurs abruptly disappeared. But the Cretaceous spanned some 65 million years. Changes in the world took place throughout this long period.

Geologically the earth had been quiet during the Jurassic. The Cretaceous was very different. All over the world great land masses sank. Shallow seas covered a greater area than ever before. Then the process reversed. Land areas began to rise again in dramatic fashion. The series of earth movements that finally resulted in our modern mountain systems like the Himalayas and the Rocky Mountains had begun.

By the end of the Cretaceous the world was a much more varied place than it had been when the dinosaurs first began to evolve.

There is some evidence that temperatures all over the world dropped slightly at the start of the Cretaceous. Then the temperatures rose again. The world at the end of the Cretaceous was probably much warmer than today's world.

The jungles in which the Jurassic dinosaurs had lived were made up of simple green plants like ferns and mosses. Some of the more dramatic changes of the Cretaceous took place in the plant world. Flowering plants and trees first arose during the Cretaceous. The last of the dinosaurs lived in woodlands that would seem very familiar to us.

In response to these changes the dinosaurs changed. The giant sauropods began to disappear. But new groups of dinosaurs came along. During the Cretaceous there were more different types of dinosaurs than ever before.

Along with the dinosaurs were snakes, lizards, and turtles. Mammals became more numerous and varied in kind. But they remained extremely small. The flying reptiles were the biggest things in the air, but true birds developed during the Cretaceous. The ichthyosaurs disappeared, but the other species of giant marine reptiles remained dominant in the sea right to the end of the Cretaceous.

So throughout the long period of the Cretaceous there were plenty of changes in the world. But every scrap of evidence that we have indicates that the dinosaurs were not dying off.

Dr. Edwin H. Colbert of the American Museum of Natural History is one of the world's leading authorities on dinosaurs. He has written, "It is a fact that the dinosaurs were quite successful up to the very end of their long reign on the earth. At no time during their existence was their success so complete or their dominance so firmly established as in the final phase of Cretaceous history. Here was the peak of dinosaurian evolution."

Yet at that very moment, when dinosaurs appeared to be most successful, they all died off. That is the mystery. We will examine some of the possible solutions in the following chapters.

IV Changing Climates

At one time both experts and non-experts alike shared a common opinion about what killed off the dinosaurs. It was believed that the earth's climate changed, and the world got cooler. The dinosaurs could not adapt to the change, so they died off. Many people, including many scientists, still hold that view.

Why would cooler temperatures have had such an effect upon the dinosaurs? The reason is that dinosaurs are believed to have been reptiles, and reptiles are cold-blooded.

The term "cold-blooded" is a bit misleading. What it means is that reptiles have no internal temperature controls. The body temperature of a reptile is controlled by the temperature of the air or water around it.

Birds and mammals, on the other hand, are warm-blooded.

That means that they possess internal temperature controls. Body heat is produced by chemical action in the cells.

We are mammals. Our body temperature is normally 98.6 degrees Fahrenheit. It remains at about 98.6 degrees whether the day is warm or cold. Only when there is something wrong with us does our body temperature go much higher or lower.

Most mammals and birds also have coverings which hold in body heat. In birds feathers serve this purpose. Most mammals have fur. We human beings have largely lost our fur. We put on clothes to hold in body heat.

On a warm, sunny day a "cold-blooded" reptile's internal temperature might actually be higher than that of a "warm-blooded" mammal. But as the temperature falls, the reptile's internal temperature falls too. If this temperature falls too low, the reptile will die. The reptile's body does not produce enough heat to control its internal temperature. Nor does a reptile have a covering like fur or feathers to hold in what little heat it does produce.

You have probably seen lizards, turtles, or snakes "sunning" themselves on warm days. These creatures are letting the sun raise their body temperature to an acceptable level. When they get warm enough, they will move off to a cooler spot. In the hot deserts many reptiles hide during the day but are active at night. When the weather gets too cool for too long, reptiles must hibernate.

Small reptiles heat up and cool down rather quickly. Large reptiles can hold a more constant temperature. It takes longer for a large object to cool down than for a smaller one. Crocodiles, giant turtles, and large lizards are able to maintain a

fairly constant temperature for days. Dinosaurs, as we all know, were the largest reptiles ever. Their immense size must have been an important factor in controlling their temperature.

But size can be a disadvantage too. While large reptiles cool down more slowly, they also heat up more slowly. Large reptiles are less susceptible to short-term, hour-to-hour changes in temperature. But they are more susceptible to longer-term changes.

In today's world large reptiles like crocodiles and giant lizards live exclusively in tropical areas. Cooler areas can support only small reptiles, and these hibernate in the winter. The cooler a region, the fewer reptiles it is likely to have. No reptiles of any size live in really cold places.

Obviously "cold-blooded" reptiles would be sharply affected by any changes in climate. If the world became substantially cooler at the end of the Cretaceous, then this would seem to be the reason why the dinosaurs died out. And for years most people simply assumed that this was the reason. They assumed this even though there was no direct evidence that such a climate change actually took place.

Determining ancient climates is not an exact science. By examining fossils of a large number of different kinds of plants and animals and studying the movements of glaciers, scientists believe that they can detect any major long-term shifts in climate. Aside from the extinction of the dinosaurs and the large marine and flying reptiles, they can find no evidence to support the theory of a major drop in temperature.

What about a rise in temperature? That too would affect the dinosaurs. While reptiles will often warm themselves in the sun, they cannot tolerate too much heat. A big increase in worldwide temperatures might also account for the extinction. But there is no indication of a sudden warming, either.

There are other objections to the climate theory. Climates had changed regularly throughout the Cretaceous. The dinosaurs had easily survived all of these changes. They had not only survived the changes, they had prospered.

A long-term climate change of even a few degrees might have had an effect upon the large dinosaurs. But not all dinosaurs were large. Besides, dinosaurs were not the only reptiles in the world. If colder or hotter weather killed off the dinosaurs, why didn't it kill off the lizards, turtles, and crocodiles?

And, finally, we must remember that dinosaurs lived all over the world. Would any change of climate have affected all parts of the world so dramatically that dinosaurs were no longer able to live anywhere? That seems unlikely.

These, then, are some of the problems with the theory that the dinosaurs died out because the world's climate changed. They do not prove that the theory is wrong, but they do make it seem less certain than it once was. When scientists stopped believing wholeheartedly in the climate theory, they began looking for other ways to explain the death of the dinosaurs.

V Habitat Change

The world in which the dinosaurs first evolved and flourished looked very different from the world from which they disappeared.

As we have said, the land surfaces of the Jurassic world were flat. Many were covered with shallow, warm seas. There was relatively little temperature change. The forests were dense and monotonously green. There were no flowering plants in the Jurassic world.

But the earth is not quiet forever. In the more than 100 million years that separate the start of the Jurassic from the end of the Cretaceous, the earth's surface shifted and folded. The result was the formation of mountain chains, and a general uplifting of the world's land surfaces. Many of the shallow seas disappeared.

Geologists call this series of changes the Laramide Revolution. "Revolution," however, is too strong a word, for it implies something sudden. These changes were millions of years in the making.

The changes in the land surface produced changes in the circulation of air and water currents. Ultimately this resulted in major shifts in climate. They certainly brought about a severe reduction in the lush, green, low-lying forests and swamps in which we like to picture dinosaurs.

But could these geographical changes and their results have brought about the death of the dinosaurs?

The major objection to this theory is that the changes came about very slowly, and the extinction of the dinosaurs came about quickly by comparison. The disappearance of the shallow seas would have restricted the range of some dinosaurs. In fact, this almost certainly caused the extinction of some species of dinosaurs like the giant sauropods. But there were others adapted to the new upland forests.

All the evidence indicates that as the world changed the dinosaurs kept right on adapting to the change. Some species died off, but new ones evolved to take advantage of the changed conditions.

Even today there are parts of South America, Africa, and Asia where dinosaurs should be able to live very well, if they did not have to compete with men or other large mammals.

There is certainly no indication of any abrupt or sudden geological activity at the end of the Cretaceous. In fact, the pace of mountain building may actually have slowed at that time.

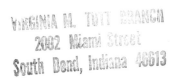

Many scientists today think that a change in plant life may hold the key to the puzzle of the death of the dinosaurs. The reason for the extinction of the large meat-eating dinosaurs is not hard to discover. Once the large plant-eating dinosaurs died out, the large meat-eating dinosaurs could not find enough food.

Such giants as Tyrannosaurus could not have survived long preying on the tiny mammals, birds, and reptiles that remained. Even the smaller predatory dinosaurs would have had a hard time without other dinosaurs to eat, though the smallest of the predatory dinosaurs could have gone on eating lizards, small mammals, and large insects, just as they always had.

So our problem is trying to figure out what happened to the plant-eating dinosaurs. A major change in plant life would, quite obviously, have had an effect upon them.

The giant plant eaters have always been something of a puzzle. In order to stay alive, they must have had to consume enormous quantities of plants. Today's large plant eaters like the elephant spend most of their waking hours searching for or consuming food. The dinosaurs were many, many times larger. Slow-moving reptiles eat less than mammals. Even if we assume (as most scientists do) that the dinosaurs needed less food per pound than modern mammals, finding food still must have presented an enormous problem. A five-ton dinosaur probably needed between 400 and 800 pounds of greenery a day.

What puzzles some scientists is that the plant eaters possessed relatively small and weak teeth. They don't look like very efficient feeders. In order to survive, they must have lived in an environment with an abundance of soft plants. But during the Cretaceous hardier, more modern plants, such as grasses, began to appear.

Today's large grass eaters like horses and cattle have large, hard teeth. Even so, a lifetime of grazing wears down their teeth badly. Dinosaurian teeth, and probably dinosaurian digestive systems, were not adapted to such rugged meals.

Yet the grasses spread slowly, and the dinosaurs continued to thrive. There is no evidence that dinosaurs ate grass or needed to. There were plenty of other plants available. The grasses did not replace older plants. They grew in areas that had once been too dry for any plants. The dinosaurs could have ignored them.

They could not have ignored other plants. Most of today's trees, shrubs, and flowering plants developed during the Cretaceous. They replaced the ferns and evergreens which had been most common. This changed the dinosaur's habitat, and presumably the dinosaur's food supply.

Recently these plants have come under increased suspicion as the culprit in the death of the dinosaurs. A British biologist, T. Swain of the Royal Botanic Gardens, says that the extinction of some 14 families of dinosaurs coincides with the rise of flowering plants.

Swain proposes that the plants evolved their own chemical protection to keep from being eaten. These chemicals developed in two stages. First came the tannins and later the alkaloids. They made the plants unattractive as food, or downright poisonous.

The early flowering plants did not contain many alkaloids but did contain tannins. These chemicals made the plants taste

bad to the dinosaurs. They were forced to range farther afield to find enough food. Often, according to this theory, they could not find enough.

Later, flowering plants with poisonous alkaloids appeared. Swain points to tests with modern reptiles which show that they cannot taste alkaloids. Mammals are sensitive to the taste of alkaloids and avoid them. If dinosaurs had taste buds like those of modern reptiles, Swain thinks that they could easily have eaten enough of the poisonous plants to kill themselves without knowing what they were doing.

As evidence, Swain points to the many dinosaur fossils found in contorted positions with head thrown back and tail curled up. These positions he says are "suggestive of alkaloid poisoning."

Another piece of evidence comes from the study of dinosaur eggs. Many fossil dinosaur eggs have been found. The shells of the eggs of late Cretaceous dinosaurs appear to be thinner than those of dinosaurs of earlier eras. This may have made them more breakable. It also may indicate that there was something wrong with the eggs and that the dinosaurs that were hatched were somehow abnormal.

In modern times the chemical pesticide DDT has produced the same sort of effect upon the eggs of many birds. It is responsible for the extinction or near extinction of a number of modern bird species. Swain thinks that alkaloids may have contributed to the thinning of the shells of dinosaur eggs.

The theory is attractive. But it runs up against some of the same problems as other theories about the extinction of the dinosaurs. The flowering plants developed slowly in a period when dinosaurs were doing very well indeed. In fact, it has been argued that the development of flowering plants gave dinosaurs new food supplies. Couldn't the dinosaurs have adapted to changes in plant life as they adapted to changes in weather and habitat?

These new plants would probably not have had any effect upon the flying reptiles, and almost certainly none on the great marine reptiles. Yet both of these died out. On the other hand, there are other plant-eating reptiles like the turtle which survived the period.

Plant poisoning may have been responsible for the death of certain types of dinosaurs. But it is difficult to see how it can be the whole answer to the question of what really happened to the dinosaurs.

VI   Competition and Disease

For over 100 million years the dinosaurs were dominant on the land. Today it is the mammals that dominate, as they have for the last 70 million years.

From that simple observation some have concluded that the mammals and the dinosaurs were in competition for food and living space. The mammals, being warm-blooded, swifter, and more intelligent, won the competition, and the dinosaurs were forced into extinction.

The theory looks good until it is examined closely. Then we realize that both the mammals and the dinosaurs evolved at about the same time. While the mammals remained small and insignificant, the dinosaurs grew into giants.

The mammals held on. They skittered unnoticed about the feet of the dinosaur giants. They may even had been eaten by some of the smaller predatory dinosaurs.

In the modern world most mammals are nocturnal—that is, active at night. This is probably an evolutionary hangover from the days of the dinosaurs. The active little mammals would come out only at night, when the big dinosaurs were asleep.

If there was any competition between the dinosaurs and the early mammals, it was the dinosaurs who were the clear winners. The great boom in mammal evolution could begin only after the dinosaurs had already died out.

There may have been a less obvious form of competition. The mammals may have been egg eaters. Many modern mammals eat the eggs of birds and reptiles. There were probably also dinosaurs that ate the eggs of other dinosaurs.

Still, it is very doubtful if this sort of egg stealing brought about the extinction of the dinosaurs. Egg stealing must have gone on for millions of years. Reptiles lay so many eggs that most of them can be eaten and a large enough percentage will still hatch to keep up the population. Egg stealing was one of the normal hazards of dinosaur life. In addition, the eggs of some of the big dinosaurs were so tough the little Cretaceous mammals probably would not have been able to break them anyway.

Another suggestion is that the dinosaurs were wiped out by a great disease epidemic. Dinosaurs were certainly susceptible to disease, as are all other living things.

In the fourteenth century an epidemic of plague known as the "Black Death" killed off one-quarter to one-third of the population of Europe. In 1918 a flu epidemic resulted in some 20 million human deaths around the world.

In the early years of the twentieth century there was a

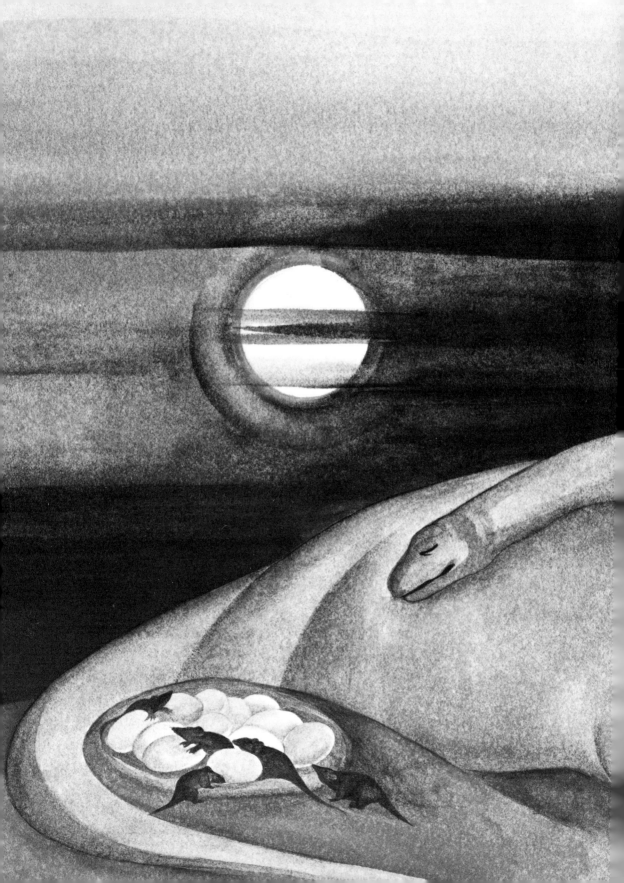

plant disease that killed nearly all of the American chestnut trees. More recently the Dutch elm disease has practically wiped out the once numerous elm trees in America.

The objection to the disease theory is that epidemics, even the worst of them, rarely kill off all the members of even one species. It is rarer still that an epidemic will strike more than one species. One can imagine an epidemic that would kill off all of the tyrannosaurs. But it simply does not fit in with what we know about epidemics to believe that the same epidemic would wipe out all the many species of duck-billed dinosaurs and all of the other dinosaurs and then carry off the marine and flying reptiles to boot.

The best that can be said for the epidemic theory is that other conditions may have weakened the dinosaurs and made them more susceptible to disease. Therefore, disease may have contributed to the extinction of the dinosaurs. But it was not the basic cause.

VII Catastrophes

Great worldwide catastrophes were once a popular way of explaining all extinctions. When people first began to discover the remains of animals that were no longer alive, they were puzzled. They wondered how all of these creatures could have died off.

No one knew how old the earth really was. Most people thought it was just a few thousand, or a few hundred thousand, years old. Less than one hundred years ago not many would have guessed that the earth is nearly 5 *billion* years old.

In order to explain how so many animals could have died out in so short a time, people assumed that the world was regularly swept by great catastrophes. The flood described in the Bible was thought to be one of these.

As scientists began to discover that the earth was far older than they had imagined, catastrophic theories became less popular. There was plenty of time for slow changes.

Geologists could find no evidence of regular worldwide catastrophes. Of course, there were catastrophes—huge floods, great volcanic eruptions, and the like. But they were local catastrophes, not worldwide events. They might kill off all life in a particular area, but they could not be held responsible for worldwide extinctions.

Still, the extinction of the dinosaurs appears so abrupt, and so unexpected, that some catastrophic theories are still popular. If the extinction of the dinosaurs was caused by a great catastrophe, it could not have been the sort we normally think of. Floods and volcanic eruptions would have left their trace in the late Cretaceous rocks. But these rocks contain no evidence that anything extraordinary happened.

A group of related theories blame the death of the dinosaurs on either a rise or fall in the amount of oxygen in the earth's atmosphere. In theory, at least, the reasons for either a rise or fall in oxygen can be explained. But the explanations are quite complicated, and need not concern us here.

There is no direct evidence at all that there was any sort of change in the earth's oxygen during late Cretaceous times. Supporters of the oxygen theory argue that such evidence would no longer exist.

But this theory faces the same objection that faced other extinction theories—why were the deaths so selective? Why all the dinosaurs, large and small, plus the marine reptiles, plus the flying reptiles? Why not the turtles and lizards and crocodiles? Surely they would have been as much affected by changes in oxygen as dinosaurs.

Even if oxygen changes up or down did take place, they would not have taken place overnight. The change would have been gradual. Dinosaurs, which had already adapted to so many changes in their world, should have been able to adapt to this change.

In recent years there has been a lot of interest in the idea that the death of the dinosaurs was brought about by radiation. We know that high doses of radiation can kill living things. Smaller doses may not produce death directly, but they can bring about changes in the reproductive cells. Radiation can make creatures sterile or produce birth defects which will cause offspring to die.

Today we think of radiation as coming from nuclear weapons, or nuclear power plants. But there is plenty of natural radiation. The earth is constantly being bombarded by radiation from space. If there were a sudden and sharp increase in this radiation from space, it would bring about widespread changes in life on earth.

Where could such a sudden increase have come from? Attention has centered upon supernovas.

A supernova is the sudden explosion of a very large star. It is a cosmic event of such size and violence that it overwhelms the earthly imagination.

In the year 1054 astronomers in China recorded the appearance of a "great star" in the sky. It faded from view after about a year. That great star was a supernova. Though it is no longer visible to the unaided eye, astronomers today can still find the remains of that supernova with their telescopes. The supernova explosion must have been a billion times brighter than our own sun. It would also have thrown off an enormous

amount of radiation. However, it took place so far from our own solar system that no harmful amounts of the radiation would ever have reached earth.

Since 1054 astronomers have observed two other supernovas. They have also identified the remains of some 200 additional supernovas with their telescopes. All of these identified supernovas were too far from our solar system to have had any effect upon it.

Most scientists believe that the supernova is an extremely rare celestial event. They reason that the probability of one taking place close enough to earth to shower radiation upon us is very, very remote. But not all scientists agree. Two Russian astronomers theorized that supernovas occur in our own galaxy about once every fifty years.

Now, a galaxy is immense. It contains billions of stars. Most of these supernovas would be nowhere near close enough to have any effect upon earth. Still, their theory holds that supernovas are about six times more common than most other scientists think. That makes it six times more likely that a supernova would occur close enough to be damaging to life on earth.

A couple of American scientists, Drs. K. D. Terry and W. Tucker, have an even more radical theory. They suggest that the radiation thrown off by a supernova would be much stronger than others believe. They estimate that the earth may be exposed to a dose of radiation high enough to cause mass extinctions once every 50 million years. The sudden burst of radiation might also cause a massive, but short-term, climate change.

There is another way in which the earth could suddenly

receive a large dose of radiation. Even without supernovas there is a lot of radiation in space. The earth is surrounded by what scientists call a magnetic "shield." No one pretends to understand how or why this shield works. But one of the things it does is protect the earth's surface from much of the radiation in space.

Scientists have found evidence that the strength of this magnetic shield changes every million years or so. During those times when the field is at its weakest point, more radiation would strike the earth. There might even be enough radiation to cause mass extinctions.

Radiation would probably do more damage to large land animals like dinosaurs than to small mammals. The mammals might spend much of their time underground in burrows where they would be protected. But why would birds be less affected than flying reptiles, and why turtles less than plesiosaurs?

No one really knows the answers to such questions. All of these theories are interesting. Perhaps they are even true. But we have no way of knowing for sure.

VIII   The Great Deaths

In addition to the dinosaurs, the great marine reptiles, and the flying reptiles, other life forms disappeared at the end of the Cretaceous. A number of groups of small marine animals either disappeared entirely or were severely reduced in numbers. Among them were the ammonites, ancient relatives of the squid and octopus, some clam-like creatures called Rudista, and some common types of one-celled animals.

Because dinosaurs are so famous, we only think of the death of the dinosaurs and of the other large reptiles. In reality, the extinctions at the end of the Cretaceous seem to have affected more than reptiles. It has been called a time of the Great Death.

There have been other periods of Great Death in the history of the earth. One of them came some 225 million years ago. It was the end of the period that geologists call the Permian. What appears to be an unusually large number of animals, big and small, suddenly disappear from the fossil record. As with the late Cretaceous extinctions, there is no evidence of a worldwide change in environment to account for these deaths.

But this period of Great Death took place long before the death of the dinosaurs. We know even less about it. There was another period of Great Death much closer to our own time. It occurred at the end of the Pleistocene (PLIS-toe-sene) period. That was only ten thousand years ago. Ten thousand years is a long time. But up until now we have been talking about millions and hundreds of millions of years.

The Pleistocene was an age of giant mammals. The giant land mammals never reached the size of the dinosaurs. They were, however, larger than any of the land mammals today. They were certainly more numerous.

Before the Pleistocene extinctions North America was the home of two species of elephants, the woolly rhinoceros, bison with a horn spread of six feet, beavers as big as bears, horses, camels, and many other large mammals. When Europeans came to North America less than 500 years ago, the only large animals they found were the bison, the moose, the grizzly bear, and, in the far north, the musk ox. Some 70 percent of all native North American mammals with a body weight of over 100 pounds disappeared at the end of the Pleistocene.

South America was hit almost as hard. Giant sloths, some of them standing 20 feet tall, had been common. The glyptodon (GLIP-toe-don), a huge, heavily-armored relative of the armadillo, had been found throughout South and Central America. It had even extended its range to the southwestern

United States. These two creatures and a host of others vanished at the end of the Pleistocene.

Europe and Asia also lost most of their large animals during this period. Africa today is the home of most of the modern world's large mammals. At first glance, it looks as though Africa's animals escaped the wave of extinctions. But this is not so. During this period Africa lost 40 percent of its large animals.

There is no obvious reason for these extinctions. As far as scientists can determine, there had been no dramatic climate change. In fact, the earth was getting warmer and should have been a better place for large mammals.

The habitat of the animals had not been destroyed. This can be demonstrated most clearly by what happened to the horse. Horses first evolved in North America. Then they migrated to Asia. North America and Asia were connected at this period. The horses died out in North and South America in the great wave of extinctions. They survived in Asia. They were domesticated and brought to Europe. Europeans brought them back to America. The American Indians were terrified of horses at first. They had never seen them before. Their ancestors must have seen living horses, but that memory was long forgotten.

When some of the European horses escaped in North America, they were easily able to adapt to living in the wild. The conditions under which they had lived were still there. Why, then, had they died out in the first place?

No one really knows. One popular theory today is that the large mammals were killed off by human hunters. According to this theory, the hunters had developed methods of killing off entire herds by driving them over cliffs with fires. It would have been a very wasteful method of hunting.

Naturally, hunting could not have accounted for the death of the dinosaurs. Nor could it have anything to do with the wave of Permian extinctions. Perhaps the Pleistocene extinctions were different from the others. And perhaps not. The hunting theory is only a theory. A good theory, to be sure, but it is a long way from being proven.

Scientists regard the development of new species and the extinction of old ones as a slow and gradual process. These periods of Great Death present problems which science has not yet been able to solve.

IX   Continuing Evolution

All along we have been assuming that the dinosaurs all died
out. We have said that there is not a single direct descendant
of the dinosaurs living today. We have also said that the dinosaurs were cold-blooded reptiles. Now we are going to have
to take another look at those statements. There are some
scientists today who say they are not correct.

No, no one has discovered a tropical island still populated
by giant dinosaurs. That has been a favorite theme of science
fiction stories and movies. Another favorite theme of science
fiction is that an atomic explosion will somehow or other "re-
vive" a frozen dinosaur, or hatch a preserved dinosaur egg.
Such ideas are fun in fiction, but there is no chance of their
happening in the real world.

Why, then, are some scientists questioning the death of the

dinosaurs? Writing in the magazine *Scientific American,* Robert T. Bakker of Harvard University stated the case quite bluntly. "The evidence suggests, in fact, that dinosaurs never died out completely. One group still lives. We call them birds."

That statement is really quite startling. We are accustomed to thinking of dinosaurs as giant reptiles, more like large lizards and crocodiles than sparrows and pigeons. Birds are small and light. But—and this we must keep in mind—so were some dinosaurs. Some even had hollow bones like birds. Scientists often commented on how bird-like many dinosaurs appeared.

Scientists divide all dinosaurs into two major orders, Saurischia (sawr-ISS-kee-ya) and Ornithischia (or-ni-THISS-kee-ya). The name Saurischia means "lizard hip" or "reptile hip." Ornithischia means "bird hip." The names refer to the formation of the hip or pelvic bones. In some dinosaurs these bones are shaped like those of modern reptiles, in others like modern birds.

So a similarity between the birds and some dinosaurs was well known. The major difference, most scientists feel, is that the dinosaurs were cold-blooded and birds are warm-blooded.

But were the dinosaurs really cold-blooded?

That is what the supporters of this new theory have begun to question. Just by looking at fossil remains there is no absolute way of telling whether a creature was warm-blooded or cold-blooded. There must be a great deal of interpretation. Since dinosaurs were first discovered, scientists assumed that they were cold-blooded because their bones most resembled those of modern reptiles. Modern reptiles *are* cold-blooded.

In the last few years some scientists have been looking at the

dinosaur with reptile hip

dinosaur with bird hip

evidence and interpreting it differently. They think that the evidence shows that the dinosaurs were warm-blooded. Their reasoning is very technical. We cannot go into it in any detail here. The question is far from settled, for the majority of scientists still hold to the traditional view that dinosaurs were reptiles and cold-blooded.

But the traditional view has been strongly challenged. Scientists at Harvard and elsewhere present a very different picture of the dinosaurs. In this new view dinosaurs were not the slow-moving, stupid creatures everyone thought they were. Not only were they warm-blooded, they were fast. Those big, armor-plated monsters didn't just lumber along; they could run when necessary. Some scientists estimate that large dinosaurs could reach speeds of 40 miles per hour.

Yes, their brains were small in comparison to the size of their bodies. But we have to remember the bodies were huge. The dinosaurs still had larger brains than the mammals of that day.

Warm-blooded dinosaurs could adapt to a far greater range of temperatures. This is one of the main arguments of those who want a new view of dinosaurs. They say that large dinosaurs lived where it was far too cold for large cold-blooded reptiles. Therefore the dinosaurs had to be warm-blooded.

The theory is attractive. It certainly helps to explain why dinosaurs were as successful as they were. Unfortunately, it makes it more difficult to explain what happened to the dinosaurs at the end of the Cretaceous.

If dinosaurs were warm-blooded, then we have good reason to consider them the ancestors of modern birds. In an earlier

Archaeopteryx

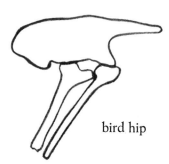

bird hip

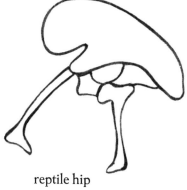

reptile hip

chapter we mentioned Archaeopteryx. This was a small reptile-like creature covered with feathers that lived about 150 million years ago. Archaeopteryx is generally considered to be the first bird, though it probably could not fly.

It was thought that both birds and dinosaurs had a common ancestor, but were not directly related. But Bakker says that the "first bird" closely resembled some small dinosaurs. In addition, other fossil dinosaurs have been found which appear to have had feathers.

The feathers, by the way, are another good argument that the dinosaurs were warm-blooded. Feathers hold in body heat. They wouldn't be necessary if there was no body heat to hold in.

If this theory is correct, then the dinosaurs were not an evolutionary dead end. They are still with us today in the form of birds. Bakker has suggested that the classification of animals should be changed. Dinosaurs should no longer be classed as reptiles. They should be put in a separate class of their own. And birds, he insists, should now be classed as dinosaurs.

So perhaps all of the dinosaurs didn't die out at the end of the Cretaceous. Some of them may be fluttering overhead right now. But that just limits the problem we started out with, it does not solve it completely. For there is no argument that a great number of dinosaurs, from tiny to gigantic, did die out suddenly at the end of the Cretaceous. And we still don't know why.

X Summing Up

We have looked at a large number of theories about the death of the dinosaurs. We have also looked at objections to every one of these theories. No single theory seems to completely explain this event.

But do we need a single explanation? No, we do not. In the view of most scientists, the extinction of the dinosaurs and the other great reptiles at the end of the Cretaceous was brought about by a combination of factors. Just what combination no one is sure.

In the last few years the word "ecology" has become very popular. The idea behind ecology is that all things, living and non-living, on this planet are connected with one another in a vast and complicated web. One element cannot be changed without affecting in some way all the other elements. Sometimes the distant effects are extremely important but difficult to determine.

Midwestern farmers spraying their crops with the pesticide DDT have helped to bring about a reduction in the number of brown pelicans in Florida. The pesticide would wash from the farmers' fields into rivers. From there it would be carried to the sea. In the sea the substance would be absorbed by the plankton, tiny animals that live in the sea. The plankton are eaten by fish, which in turn are eaten by the pelicans. When the DDT gets into the bodies of the pelicans, it causes them to lay eggs with thinner shells. These eggs break easily, and thus fewer pelicans are hatched.

This is a relatively simple example. It has happened in the modern world. DDT is a man-made substance, and easily traceable. We know the process by which it was transferred from the farmers' fields to the pelicans. But if it had all happened millions of years ago, there would be no obvious way of connecting the introduction of DDT with the reduction in the number of pelicans.

In thinking about this problem, we must always remind ourselves of the immense amounts of time that are involved. The death of the dinosaurs took place over 70 million years ago. The extinctions may have stretched out over a period of several hundred thousand years. The geological record does not allow any finer distinctions. A few species may have died out every century or so.

In the present century over 100 species of animals and birds have already become extinct. The ultimate cause of practically all of these extinctions is human activity. But there were many different immediate causes. In some cases extinctions were brought about by the introduction of poisonous substances like DDT. In other cases it was the destruction of habitats. In still others hunting was the cause. Often these factors worked in combination with one another.

If this pattern of extinctions continues for several hundred more years, the world will have once again experienced a period of Great Death. Yet there can be no single massive catastrophe to account for the extinctions. Unless one considers the emergence of modern man as a catastrophe.

The evidence we have about the world of 70 million years ago is scanty and fragmentary. Therefore the problem of what really happened to the dinosaurs will provoke disagreements and puzzlement among scientists for a long time to come. It is one of those problems that may never be solved to everyone's satisfaction. But that doesn't make it any less fascinating.

SUGGESTED READING

FOR YOUNG READERS

Colbert, Edwin H. *The Dinosaur Book*. New York: McGraw-Hill, 1951.

Craig, M. Jean. *Dinosaurs and More Dinosaurs*. New York: Four Winds Press, 1968.

McGowen, Tom. *Album of Dinosaurs*. Chicago: Rand McNally & Company, 1972.

Pringle, Laurence. *Dinosaurs and Their World*. New York: Harcourt Brace Jovanovich, Inc., 1968.

FOR OLDER READERS

Desmond, Adrian J. *The Hot-Blooded Dinosaurs*. New York: The Dial Press, 1976.

INDEX

Italic number indicates illustration

Daniel Cohen has written over fifty books, including *The Ancient Visitors*, *Supermonsters*, and *Ghostly Animals*. While doing research for *What Really Happened to the Dinosaurs?*, he realized how current the study of dinosaurs still is. Many new theories developed over the last few years may completely alter our view of these huge animals.

Mr. Cohen has a degree in journalism from the University of Illinois. He lives in Port Jervis, New York.

Haru Wells illustrated *The Master Puppeteer* by Katherine Paterson, winner of the 1977 National Book Award for Children's Literature. She also illustrated *The Way of Our People* by Arnold A. Griese and *Of Nightingales That Weep* by Katherine Paterson. Ms. Wells, who was born in Buenos Aires, now lives in Dallas, Texas.